Osvaldo Golijov

Deaths of the Angel

T0056539

for String Ensemble
(from Last Round)

Full Score
Archive Edition

HENDON MUSIC

BOOSEY & HAWKES

AN IMAGEM COMPANY

DISTRIBUTED BY

HAL•LEONARD®
CORPORATION
7777 W. BLUEMOUND RD. P.O. BOX 13819 MILWAUKEE, WI 53213

www.boosey.com
www.halleonard.com

Published by Hendon Music, Inc.
a Boosey & Hawkes company
229 West 28th Street, 11th Floor
New York NY 10001

www.boosey.com

 AN IMAGEM COMPANY

© Copyright 2001 by Hendon Music, Inc.
a Boosey & Hawkes company.
Copyright for all Countries. All rights Reserved.

First Printing, 2001
Second Printing, 2009
Third Printing with updated imprint page, 2011

Position of the Players

(violins, violas and contrabass should be standing)

Contrabass

Violoncello A   Violoncello B

Viola A   Viola B

Violin IIA   Violin IIB

Violin IA   Violin IB

AUDIENCE

This work can be performed in 3 different ways, depending on the size of the string ensemble.

1. 9 players. Any indications pertaining to soli and tutti should be ignored.

2. *Small string orchestra* (larger than 9 players). The first movement should be played by 9 players; the tutti should join in starting with the second movement. Any indications in the first movement pertaining to soli or tutti should be ignored.

3. *Large string orchestra.* The first movement's indications for soli and tutti should be observed. The ideal number of players for a large orchestra is 12-8-6-4 for each "quartet" group and 6 bass players. When performed this way, it may be desirable to place the soloists in front of the main sections, close to the conductor.

In addition, the second movement may be played by itself, as a separate piece.

Program Note

Astor Piazzolla, the last great Tango composer, was at the peak of his creativity when a stroke killed him in 1992. He left us, in the words of the old tango, "without saying good bye", and on that day the musical face of Buenos Aires was abruptly frozen. The creation of that face had started a hundred years ago from the unlikely combination of African rhythms underlying gauchos' couplets, sung in the style of Sicilian canzonettas over an accompanying Andalucian guitar. As the years passed, all converged towards the bandoneon: a small accordion-like instrument without keyboard that was invented in Germany in the nineteenth century to serve as a portable church organ and which, after finding its true home in the bordellos of Buenos Aires' slums in the 1920's, went back to Europe to conquer Paris' high society in the 1930's. Since then it reigned as the essential instrument for any Tango ensemble.

Piazzolla's bandoneon was able to condense all the symbols of tango. The eroticism of legs and torsos in the dance was reduced to the intricate patterns of his virtuoso fingers (a simple C major scale in the bandoneon zigzags so much as to leave an inexperienced player's fingers tangled). The melancholy of the singer's voice was transposed to the breathing of the bandoneon's continuous opening and closing. The macho attitude of the tangueros was reflected in his pose on stage: standing upright, chest forward, right leg on a stool, the bandoneon on top of it, being by turns raised, battered, caressed.

I composed *Last Round* (the title is borrowed from a short story on boxing by Julio Cortázar) as an imaginary chance for Piazzolla's spirit to fight one more time. The piece is conceived as an idealized bandoneon. There are two movements: the first represents the act of a violent compression of the instrument and the second a final, seemingly endless opening sigh (it is actually a fantasy over the refrain of the song "My Beloved Buenos Aires", composed by the legendary Carlos Gardel in the 1930's). But *Last Round* is also a sublimated tango dance. Two quartets confront each other, separated by the focal bass, with violins and violas standing up as in the traditional tango orchestras. The bows fly in the air as inverted legs in crisscrossed choreography, always attracting and repelling each other, always in danger of clashing, always avoiding it with the immutability that can only be acquired by transforming hot passion into pure pattern.

OSVALDO GOLIJOV

To my friends Geoff Nuttall and Barry Shiffman

Commissioned by Birmingham Contemporary Music Group with financial assistance from West Midlands Arts and the following Sound Investors through BCMG's Sound Investment scheme:

Catherine & Derrick Archer, John & Bobbie Clugston, Sue Clugston, Alan Cook, Sue Grace, Richard Hartree, Stephen Johnson & Deborah Richardson, John A R & Joyce M Pollock, Howard & Sue Skempton, Michael B. Squires, Adam Watson & Jeremy Lindon, Judith Weir, Pat & Marjorie Welch

First Performances: BCMG, under the direction of Stefan Asbury
October 25, 1996. Sir Adrian Boult Hall, Birmingham
October 27, 1996: Jacqueline Du Pré Concert Hall, Oxford
December 5, 1996: Symphony Hall, Birmingham

Muertes Del Angel
Deaths of the Angel

Osvaldo Golijov
(* 1960)

© Copyright 2001 by Hendon Music, Inc.

a Boosey & Hawkes company.

Copyright for all Countries. All rights Reserved.

rit.

7 **Lentisimo, como al principio, grave**